DAREDEVILS

TANK COMMANDER

by Bill Holder

Willowisp Press®

*To the soldiers of the 5th Squadron,
12th Cavalry Regiment, Fort Knox, Kentucky*

Photos by John Farquhar
and the Department of Defense Stillmedia

Published by Willowisp Press, Inc.
401 E. Wilson Bridge Road, Worthington, Ohio 43085

Copyright © 1990 by Willowisp Press, Inc.

All rights reserved. No portion of this book may be reproduced, stored in a retrieval system, or transmitted, in any form or by any means, electronic, mechanical, photocopying, recording or otherwise without prior written permission from the publisher.

Printed in the United States of America

10 9 8 7 6 5 4 3 2 1

ISBN 0-87406-473-2

CONTENTS

A Metal Monster 4
The M1 Abrams Tank 8
The M1 Team 14
The Tank Commander 16
The Gunner 19
The Driver 20
The Loader 21
Battle Plan! 22
More Army Armor 28
Being the Best 30
Glossary 31
Index 32

A METAL MONSTER

From your perch on top of the turret, you look around the countryside. The sun is just coming up. About 50 yards away, in some trees, you see another metal monster, just like yours. You nod to the man sitting in the turret.

Now you look around at your machine. It's an awesome 60-ton combination of Ferrari and Bigfoot, a sports car and a monster truck—with a whole lot of firepower thrown in! Your machine is one of the most devastating weapons in the U.S. Army—the M1 battle tank.

You've got a great crew. You've been through a lot together and you've become like a family. Next to you is the loader, who makes sure the big gun is ready to fire when needed. And inside the tank is the gunner. He fires the big gun, and he's also the number two man, the one who takes over if anything happens to you. Down in front is the driver, who can make this huge machine turn on a dime.

And you're the man who gives orders. You make the life and death decisions. You're the tank commander.

Have you ever wanted to be the commander of a battle tank? This book will let you survey the battlefield from the turret of the most powerful tank in the world, the U.S. Army M1. You'll command the crew, as your tank roars across country at a breathtaking 45 miles an hour. You'll try to hang on to your helmet as the M1 climbs up a four-foot hill and crosses a nine-foot ditch. And when the mighty 120mm cannon fires its shells, you'll feel it in your bones and your gut.

You've heard them say, "When the going gets tough, the tough get going." Well, it doesn't get much tougher than ripping cross-country over rough, battle-scarred terrain in a giant metal monster. Let's meet this amazing machine and the tough guys who make it work.

THE M1 ABRAMS TANK

The first tanks were built by the British for the trench warfare of World War I. While early tanks were fat, ugly little creatures compared to today's sleek, speedy machines, the basic idea is the same—a protected, rolling cannon on track wheels.

The idea of tanks caught on, and they have been used with devastating results in every war since. Tanks are considered one of the most important and versatile weapons in armies around the world today.

The M1 Abrams, named after the U.S. commander in Vietnam, is a race car among the world's tanks. Powered by its smooth 1500-horsepower jet turbine engine, it has a top speed over level ground of 45 miles an hour. It's not fast compared to a car or motorcycle. But remember, this beast weighs in at 60 tons, as much as about 30 small cars!

The M1 has what's called a low vehicle silhouette, which makes it harder for the enemy to see. But its big gun can still toss a 120mm shell weighing 16 pounds up to 36 miles. How big is a 120mm shell? It's about as thick as a one-liter bottle of pop—but longer.

You probably won't be surprised to learn that the M1 gets less than a mile a gallon. But it can carry almost 500 gallons of fuel, giving it a range of about 300 miles. And thanks to the motor's simplified design, you only have to bring your M1 in for an engine overhaul every 12,000 miles. That's a huge improvement over earlier tanks.

Covered with the latest in protective armor and equipped with an awesome variety of guns and electronic equipment, the M1 is king of the battlefield. It's designed to run around, smash over, crash through, or blow up anything in its way!

THE M1 TEAM

Even a machine as awesome as the M1 is only as good as its crew. And the army puts only the best people in its best tank. Each of the four crew members has a special job to do. But they've got to learn to think as one. Each person has to know what the other is doing all the time.

"It's where we live, sleep, and eat," explained one tank crew member. "We really get to know each other."

As commander, you're the one who has to create that feeling of family closeness that the best crews have. You've been through a lot together, from your basic tank training at Army Armor School in Fort Knox, Kentucky, to the qualification test you have to pass every six months. You've spent a lot of 12-hour days together in that tank. Your crew's togetherness didn't come easy.

But then, you didn't expect it to be easy. You wouldn't want it any other way.

THE TANK COMMANDER

You're in charge—it's as simple as that. You make the decisions. Your position is looking out of a hatch on top of the turret. Sure, it's a great view, but it does get a little rough sometimes. But you're not sitting there for the view. You've got a job to do.

In front of you is your personal weapon, a 50-caliber machine gun. You've also got a thermal viewer, for finding targets in bad weather or at night, and a position navigation system, to show you where you are at all times.

You keep in radio contact with the other members of your crew. The radios come in handy when things get messy and noisy. You're also in contact with the other tanks in your battle group, or platoon. A platoon of tanks has a Platoon Leader, who's the commander for all the tanks in the unit. He's out in the field, close to the action, in his own tank.

THE GUNNER

Number two in command is the gunner. He's down inside the tank. As you can guess, it's pretty cramped down there. His job is to use the M1's incredible battery of electronic aiming systems to lock on to the enemy target. Day or night, good weather or bad, fog or smoke—it doesn't matter. The tank's computer and laser help the gunner aim and fire.

THE DRIVER

Half lying down, with his head peeping out below the main gun, is the driver. Surprisingly, the giant M1 tank uses a steering system that's a little like a motorcycle's. It's the driver's job to learn how to use the tank's quickness and speed on the battlefield. With six different speeds in the M1's transmission, you don't learn how to drive one of these in an hour or two.

THE LOADER

Up on top, next to the commander, sits the loader, with another machine gun. The loader's got to be good—he's the one who keeps the main gun loaded and ready to fire. And if the big gun's not loaded, even the best commander in the world can't make it fire! The best loaders can have the next round ready in five seconds.

BATTLE PLAN!

Climb into the turret, strap on your helmet and radio set, and let's take the M1 out into the field. Your crew is ready. Everything checks out. The metal monster roars to life. The first thing you notice is the loud, smelly tank of the past is gone. The M1's jet turbine engine is smooth and quiet, with power to spare.

Like most modern weapons, the M1 is loaded with complex electronic equipment. This equipment does many things. It helps the gunner aim and fire, even if he can't see the targets. It helps him lock on to the targets, even when the tank is moving. And because the main gun can bend a little from the heat of firing its shells, the M1 even has a special system to bring back the accuracy of the gun.

Your crew members wear uniforms made of a special fire-resistant material. A fire in a tank can spell disaster, and crews have to practice escaping from a burning tank. A line on the back of each crew member's uniform shows rescuers where to attach a rope if they have to lift an injured crew member out of a burning tank.

In your M1 you can cross ditches and boulder fields, smash through fences, forests, and other barriers, speed through storms of bullets, fire, and poison gas, and even swim through streams and small lakes.

25

Even though your tank can move like lightning across the countryside, it's still a big target for the enemy. But you've got some tricks up your sleeve to protect your M1.

For one thing, with your camouflage netting and paint, as well as your smokeless turbine engine, you're pretty hard to see. Plus, you've got the most up-to-date tank armor. It's strongest on the front, so you're taught to keep the front of the tank pointing toward the enemy lines. This protects the sides and back of the tank, where the armor is thinner.

You can also create a screen of thick smoke from your engine to hide from the enemy, or set off smoke grenades to give you time to escape to safety.

To guard against fire, your tank has a system of fire extinguishers. The fuel tanks and the ammunition are protected by armor. The M1 can also be sealed off from the outside, providing your crew with fresh, filtered air, in case the enemy uses chemical warfare.

MORE ARMY ARMOR

No matter how powerful the M1 is, it still needs several important support vehicles to help it do its job. One of them is the M113 Armored Personnel Carrier (top right). It can carry 12 soldiers at speeds of up to 40 miles per hour.

The M106A2 Mortar Carrier, the M109A3 Howitzer (below), and the M3A1 Bradley Fighting Vehicle (bottom right) all have large anti-tank cannons or missiles that are used against enemy armor. Working together with the M1, these vehicles make up a powerful team that can overcome any obstacle.

BEING THE BEST

You're four people, with one goal—to make your team the best. All four of you have to know your jobs inside and out. You've got to know the equipment so well you could operate it in your sleep. And you have to work together like clockwork.

You're the guy who has to make all this happen. You're the one the crew looks to to make the goal a reality. But when the crew does come together and reach its goal of being number one, you know it's because of you. You're in charge—nobody else.

You're a tank commander.

INDEX

armor, 13, 26
armor support vehicles, 28, 29
camouflage, 26, 31
chemical warfare, 27, 31
commander, 5, 6, 16, 17, 18
driver, 5, 20
engine, 10
Fort Knox, Kentucky, 14
gunner, 5, 19
laser, 19
loader, 5, 21

machine gun, 17, 21
position navigation system, 17
platoon, 18
shells, 120 mm, 6, 11, 23
smoke grenades, 27
tanks, early, 8
thermal viewer, 17
uniforms, 24
Vietnam, 10
World War I, 8

GLOSSARY

camouflage Using special paint, netting, and other things to make the tank hard to see.

chemical warfare A terrible type of war in which poison gas is used to harm enemy soldiers.

low vehicle silhouette This means the M1 is low and close to the ground, making it hard for the enemy to see and destroy.

platoon A group of tanks working together in a battle. A platoon has an overall tank commander.

thermal viewer A special viewer that detects the heat that objects give off. This helps the tank's crew find and destroy targets when they can't see them.

track The "wheels" of a tank, which are well suited for going over rough terrain. Wheels on the inside turn a continuous track with large treads for good traction.

turbine engine A powerful engine that gets its power from a turning part called a rotor. The M1 uses a jet turbine engine.

turret The top part of a tank where the commander and loader sit and the main gun comes out. The turret rotates.